Ripley's Believe It or Not!

Developed and produced by Ripley Publishing Ltd

This edition published and distributed by:
Mason Crest Publishers Inc.
370 Reed Road, Broomall, Pennsylvania 19008
(866) MCP-BOOK (toll free)
www.masoncrest.com

Ripley's Believe it or Not!
Breaking Boundaries
ISBN 978-1-4222-2016-0 (hardcover)
ISBN 978-1-4222-2050-4 (paperback)

Library of Congress Cataloging-in-Publication data is available

Ripley's Believe it or Not!—Complete 16 Title Series
ISBN 978-1-4222-2014-6

1st printing
10 9 8 7 6 5 4 3 2 1

Library of Congress Cataloging-in-Publication Data is available.
Printed in USA

PUBLISHER'S NOTE
While every effort has been made to verify the accuracy of the entries in this book, the
Publisher's cannot be held responsible for any errors contained in the work. They would
be glad to receive any information from readers.

WARNING
Some of the stunts and activities in this book are undertaken by experts and should not
be attempted by anyone without adequate training and supervision.

Expect... The Unexpected

Mason Crest Publishers

BREAKING BOUNDARIES

On the edge. If you think you can push yourself to

the limit you won't be so sure when you take a look

inside. Read about the woman who wore a corset

for over 20 years, the man who can eat 49 hot dogs

in just 12 minutes, and the 9-mi (14-km)

gum wrapper chain.

Robert Jones of Pine Bluff, Arkansas, practices
his "thumb-stands" on juggling pins...

Building Ace

FOR ALMOST 20 years, Bryan Berg has been creating some of the world's most famous buildings from playing cards. At the 2005 Canada National Exhibition in Toronto, the celebrated cardstacker amazed audiences with his detailed replicas of the Taj Mahal, the Colosseum, and the Pyramids.

Berg bases his card towers on carefully constructed grids. He says that the combined weight of the cards actually adds to the stability of the structure.

Berg, who comes from Spirit Lake, Iowa, was introduced to cardstacking by his grandfather at the age of eight. By the time he was 17, Berg was building towers of cards over 14 ft (4.3 m) tall. In 1999, he built a 133-story tower that was 25 ft (7.6 m) high from 2,000 packs of cards. He needed scaffolding so that he could reach the very top. In February 2005, as part of the Asian tsunami relief effort, Berg worked for 18 hours a day, ten days straight, to construct a skyline of New York City. He used 178,000 playing cards, each of which represented a victim of the disaster. The Empire State Building, the Chrysler Building, and Yankee Stadium were all there in breathtaking accuracy.

Berg puts the finishing touches to a Gothic cathedral.

The Taj Mahal stands in the foreground with Rome's Colosseum behind. Berg never uses adhesives. "There are no tricks," he adds. "It's all in the balancing."

Berg demonstrated a refreshing anarchy toward his art on the final night of his Canadian spectacle by enthusiastically destroying his patiently created work with a gas-powered leaf blower!

7

Air Guitar

At the 2005 Guilfest music festival in Guildford, England, 4,083 people gathered to play air guitars at the same time. With air-guitar "experts" on hand to dispense advice, the wannabee rockers mimed to "Sweet Child of Mine" by Guns 'n' Roses.

Eggs Galore

At the annual Easter egg hunt at Rockford, Illinois, on March 26, 2005, an incredible 292,686 eggs were hunted for and found by 1,500 children in just 15 minutes. The event involved 200 volunteers, 156 bales of straw, and 1,000 hours of stuffing plastic eggs.

⊽ Eggstraordinary

Brian Spott from Colorado balanced 439 eggs on the floor at Melbourne's Australian Centre for Contemporary Art in 2005. He said the secret was to find the sweet spot on the base of an egg, adding: "You need a steady hand and a lot of patience."

Modern Houdini

Canadian escape artist Dean Gunnarson specializes in freeing himself from handcuffs and locked coffins. One of his most famous routines is the "Car Crusher," which he performed in Los Angeles, California, in 1990. First he was handcuffed and then chained into a 1970 Cadillac by the South Pasadena Chief of Police. Gunnarson's neck was chained to the steering wheel, his legs were bound to the brake pedal, and his arms fastened to the doors. The Cadillac was then lifted into a car crusher, which was set into motion, its steel jaws closing menacingly. A mere 2 minutes 7 seconds later, Gunnarson amazingly leapt to freedom from his automobile prison, just a few seconds before the vehicle was completely destroyed by the merciless crusher.

Plane Sailing

Canada's Ken Blackburn is no regular aviator—he deals strictly in paper airplanes. He has been making paper planes since the age of ten and broke his first record in 1983, when he managed to keep his creation airborne for 16.89 seconds. But he bettered that at the Georgia Dome, Atlanta, in 1998 with an unbeatable 27.6 seconds.

At Seattle's 2005 Northwest Folklife Festival, Andy Mackie led no fewer than **1,706 harmonica** players in a 13 min 22 sec rendition of "Twinkle, Twinkle Little Star."

Voice Broke

Terry Coleman of Denver, Colorado, sang continuously for 40 hours 17 minutes in July 2005. His target was 49 hours, but his voice gave out after 40. "The hardest thing was staying awake," he said afterward.

Wheelchair Star

In July 2005, neuroscientist William Tan from Singapore covered 151 mi (243 km) in a wheelchair in just 24 hours by completing a staggering 607 laps of an athletics track. Two months earlier, the redoubtable Tan had completed 6½ marathons on seven continents in the space of only 70 days.

▶ Lip Stick

Joseph Cervantez of Gurnee, Illinois, makes contact, puckering his lips up for an uninterrupted kiss lasting 7 hours 43 minutes on February 14, 2005. He beat rival Juan Hyde and won a new truck worth $32,235 for his achievement.

Unicycle Feats

Between 1976 and 1978, Wally Watts of Edmonton, Canada, rode a unicycle 12,000 mi (19,300 km) in various countries around the world. And through 1983 to 1984, Pierre Biondo of Montreal, Canada, rode a unicycle around the entire perimeter of North America, just over 12,000 mi (19,300 km).

Hula Heroine

Australian circus performer Kareena Oates created history in June 2005 by managing to spin 100 hula hoops around her waist for three full revolutions.

◀ Pulling Teeth

In June 1999, 36-year-old Krishna Gopal Shrivestava pulled a 270-ton boat a distance of 49 ft (15 m) in Calcutta harbor using only his teeth.

Birthday Bowl

Seventy-year-old Jean Beal bowled 70 games in one day (one game for each year of her life), on June 29, 2005, to celebrate her birthday. It took her nearly 14 hours. Jean, from Hickory, North Carolina, said of the challenge: "I was just doing it to see if I could."

The One that Got Away

In May 2005, Tim Pruitt of Alton, Illinois, caught a record 124-lb (56-kg) blue catfish in the Mississippi River. The monster-sized fish measured a staggering 58 in (147 cm) long and 44 in (112 cm) around. Alas, the fish, which was thought to be at least 30 years old, died the following week while being transported to a Kansas City aquarium where it was to go on public display.

▷ Happy Birthday!

An incredible 27,413 birthday candles lit up New York City on August 27, 2005. Taking 1½ minutes, 50 people rapidly lit candles on top of a cake that measured 47 x 3 ft (14 x 0.9 m).

Backward Bowler

Jim Cripps isn't content with bowling scores of over 250—he does it backwards! It all started as a joke. Jim, from Nashville, Tennessee, was clowning around at the lanes one afternoon when he suddenly made a decision to bowl backwards. He turned his back on the pins, took a few steps, hurled the ball and got a strike! One of his friends bet him he couldn't bowl a 150 in reverse, but after six weeks of practice, Jim managed it. Bowling backwards, he rolled a 279 in a game that included 11 consecutive strikes.

Blind Date

In July 2005, Singapore's Nanyang Technological University staged a romantic event as part of its 50th anniversary celebrations, whereby 536 first-year undergraduates (268 couples) got together to stage a mass blind date.

Large Deposit

In June 2005, Edmond Knowles walked up to a Coinstar machine at a bank in Flomaton, Alabama, and cashed in 1,308,459 pennies, which amounted to $13,084.59. He had started saving pennies in 1967, keeping the coins in a 5-gal (19-l) can. But, by the time of his huge deposit, he had collected so many that they were being stored in four large 55-gal (208-l) drums and three 20-gal (76-l) drums.

Hockey Marathon

In June 2005, Canadian radio host Mike Nabuurs played air hockey for 48 hours straight, at a table in the lobby of McMaster University Medical Center, Hamilton, Ontario.

◁ Ice Statue

Russian Karim Diab stood motionless in the freezing Moscow River for one whole hour. He had prepared for two years to accustom his body to surviving in the icy water for an hour without moving. He recovered with a hot bath, but was still too cold to talk.

Fastest Fingers

Dean Gould of Felixstowe, England, can lay claim to being amazingly dexterous. For over 20 years the 46-year-old father-of-three has shown that he has the fastest fingers and the handiest hands by setting new standards in such reaction-testing skills as beer-coaster flipping, winkle picking, pancake tossing, coin snatching, and needle threading.

Tongue-tied

Using only his tongue, Florida firefighter Al Gliniecki tied 39 cherry stems into knots in three minutes in 1999. On another occasion, he tied an incredible 833 stems in one hour. Yet Al nearly wasn't around to put his talented tongue to use. While working as a lifeguard at Pensacola in 1982, he was struck by a bolt of lightning that threw him 38 ft (12 m) and blew the fillings out of his teeth.

Ballpark Marathon

In 2005, Mike Wenz and Jake Lindhorst saw 30 baseball games in 29 days—each in a different major-league ballpark. The 22-year-old buddies from Chicago began their ballpark marathon in New York's Shea Stadium on June 12 and finished at Miami's Dolphin Stadium on July 10.

Wrap Artist

ON MARCH 11, 1965, a 14-year-old Canadian boy stuck a wad of Wrigley's gum in his mouth and carefully folded the wrappers into links. That night he scribbled an entry in his diary: "I started my gum-wrapper chain with 20 spearmint gum wrappers today."

Forty years later, Gary Duschl's gum-wrapper chain is made up of over one million wrappers and stretches for more than 47,000 ft (14,325 m)—9 mi (14.5 km)—at his home in Virginia Beach, Virginia. To travel the length of the chain would take 9 minutes in a car traveling at 60 mph (97 km/h)! What started out as a desire to have the longest chain in class, then in school, then in the area, has become a 630-lb (285-kg) monster. There is more than $50,000-worth of gum in Duschl's incredible chain.

Many of the wrappers are sent in by well-wishers. Duschl admits that even he couldn't have chewed that amount of gum during the past four decades!

Sky High
To celebrate her 99th birthday on February 17, 1996, Hildegarde Ferrera made a parachute jump over Hawaii. She came through the jump with nothing worse than a sore neck, but sadly died two weeks later from pneumonia.

Most people would use a 14-oz (400-g) bottle of ketchup sparingly. Not **Dustin Phillips** from Los Angeles, California. In 1999, he drank 90 per cent of a bottle through a straw in just 33 seconds (and wasn't sick)!

Handstand Display
A total of 1,072 people turned up at Indianapolis in 2005 to perform an astonishing display of simultaneous handstands. Participants in the challenge came from as far afield as Kansas, Texas, and Oregon.

 Get the Picture
Australian artist Ando has created a huge painting of the outback, which measures an amazing 328 x 39 ft (100 x 12 m). Painted on a curved canvas, "The Big Picture" is complemented by more than 300 tons of red landscaped earth (see right), which adds to the image's 3-D effect. Only from certain angles are visitors able to see where 2-D meets 3-D.

Short Story
Adeel Ahmed, a 24-year-old Pakistani seen here being interviewed, is only 37 in (94 cm) high. He was born a normal child, but by the age of five had stopped growing.

Giant Skis
In February 2005, in Jacques Cartier Park in Ottawa, Ontario, 100 skiers traveled 330 ft (100 m) on a gigantic pair of skis, 330 ft (100 m) long.

Check Mates
An incredible 12,388 players turned out to take part in simultaneous chess matches at a public park in Pachuca, near Mexico City, one day in June 2005. Around 80 per cent of the competitors were children.

Long Train
When Hege Lorence married Rolf Rotset in Norway in June 1996, her bridal train was 670 ft (204 m) long, and had to be carried by 186 bridesmaids and pageboys.

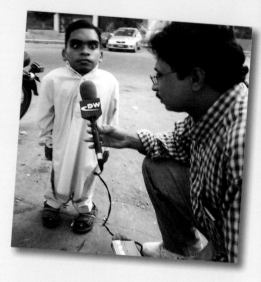

Delicious Worms
"Snake" Manohoran, a 23-year-old hotelier from Madras, India, ate 200 earthworms in 30 seconds in 2004. He said that he overcame any reservations about eating them by simply thinking of them as meat. He acquired the nickname from his trick of putting his pet snake up his nose and pulling it out through his mouth!

Icy Voyage
After chasing a coyote on the ice near Canada's Prince Edward Island in 2001, foxhound Scooter was carried out to sea in a blizzard. She was rescued five days later after traveling 43 mi (70 km) on an ice floe across the Northumberland Strait.

Whip-cracker

Illinois entertainer Chris Camp cracked a 6 ft (1.8 m) bullwhip 222 times in one minute on the Mike Wilson Show in April 2005!

Child Prodigy

Michael Kearney did not sleep as much as other babies. Instead, he just wanted to talk. By the age of just five months, he was using four-word sentences, and at six months he calmly told a pediatrician: "I have a left-ear infection." He enrolled at Santa Rosa Junior College when he was just six years old and graduated two years later with an Associate of Science in Geology. In 1994, aged ten, he received a bachelor's degree in Anthropology from the University of South Alabama. He achieved a master's degree in Chemistry at 14 and was teaching in college at the tender age of 17.

High Flyers

A team from Edmonds Community College, Washington State, flew a kite continuously for more than 180 hours (7½ days) at nearby Long Beach in August 1982.

▶ More than a Mouthful

This appetite-buster hamburger, made by Denny's Beer Barrel Pub in Clearfield, Pennsylvania, on June 1, 2004, weighed about 11 lb (4.9 kg).

Twisted Walk

Inspired by an item on the *Ripley's Believe It or Not!* TV show, an Indian teenager has perfected the art of walking with his heels twisted backward. Despite misgivings from his mother that he might injure his legs, Bitu Gandhi from Rajkot in the state of Gujarat practiced until he was able to walk 300 steps forward and 300 steps backward by twisting his ankles nearly 180 degrees.

TV Addicts

Believe it or not, Chris Dean, 16, and Mike Dudek, 17, from Grand Rapids, Michigan, watched television for 52 hours nonstop in August 2004!

TIGHTROPE WALKER
Clifford Calverley, of Toronto, Canada, crossed Niagara Falls on a steel cable in 1892, taking just 6 minutes 32 seconds.

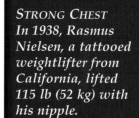

STRONG CHEST
In 1938, Rasmus Nielsen, a tattooed weightlifter from California, lifted 115 lb (52 kg) with his nipple.

GIANT CHAIR
Built in 1934 by W.E. Houston of Orlando, Florida, this chair measured 26 ft (8 m) high by 12 ft (3.7 m) wide by 8 ft (2.5 m) deep, and weighed 1,400 lb (635 kg).

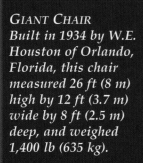

EYE-OPENER
Ever wanted a beer but couldn't find the opener? Bob Oldham of South Carolina was able to remove bottle tops with his eyes!

MISSISSIPPI MARATHON
Long-distance swimmer Fred Newton of Clinton, Oklahoma, swam an incredible 2,300 mi (3,700 km) down the Mississippi River in 1931.

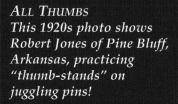

ALL THUMBS
This 1920s photo shows Robert Jones of Pine Bluff, Arkansas, practicing "thumb-stands" on juggling pins!

HEAD TO TOE
Myra Jeanne of Buffalo, New York, specialized in tap dancing on her own head.

PRICKLY MATTRESS
This photograph of a young boy lying on a bed of nails was taken by missionary W.E. Morton in Benares, India, in 1926.

Looking Back

August 14, 1934 **Lee Chisman**, from Danville, Kentucky, was known as the "Big Bellow Man" because his voice could be heard from 8 mi (13 km) away. **October 11, 1942** **Warren Moore** from Jennings Lodge, Oregon, played 240 notes in one breath on the tuba. **May 20, 1952** **Myrtle Bliven**, aged 70, crocheted five tiny hats that could rest side by side on a single dime.

Sweet Treat

Jim Hager, a dental-plan manager from Oakland, California, ate 115 M&M's® with a pair of chopsticks in just 3 minutes in September 2003.

Endurance Test

Cathie Llewellyn of Wintersville, Ohio, won a new car in 2005 after living in the vehicle for 20 days. She triumphed when her last remaining opponent gave up because she needed to use the bathroom. All contestants had been allowed a five-minute break every six hours during the challenge, which took place in a Steubenville, Ohio, shopping mall.

Fast Fingers

Barbara Blackburn, of Salem, Oregon, can type 150 words per minute for 50 minutes (37,500 key strokes), and has a top speed of 212 words per minute and an error frequency of just 0.002 per 100 words. Her secret is a special keyboard, which has vowels on one side and consonants on the other.

⏷ Ear We Go

Lash Pataraya from Georgia, lifted 115 lb (52 kg) with his ears in Tbilisi in October 2003. He also used his ears to pull a minibus weighing 1½ tons a distance of 158 ft (48 m), by attaching it to his ears with string.

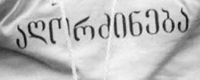

⏶ Using Your Loaf

In August 2005, in the small town of Mottola, Italy, a monster focaccia was baked. Measuring 78 x 41 ft (23.7 x 12.5 m), the traditional flat bread covered an area of 3,200 sq ft (297 sq m). It was baked in a special wood-and-coal burning oven 4,840 sq ft (450 sq m) wide. The cooked focaccia weighed an estimated 62,000 lbs (28,000 kg) and was consumed by 40,000 spectators.

A Knife's Edge

The Great Throwdini is a world-champion knife-throwing minister from Freeport, New York, who takes the world of "impalement arts" to the extreme with his death-defying Maximum Risk act.

When and why did you become a knife thrower?

❝My real name is the Rev. Dr. David Adamovich and for 18 years I was a professor of exercise physiology. When I was 50, I opened a pool hall and one of my customers brought in a small throwing knife. I threw it into a tree outside and struck it perfectly. Nine months later I came second in the world knife-throwing championship.❞

What is Maximum Risk?

❝I'm one of the world's best in competition throwing, and I've converted that skill into a stage act called Maximum Risk. The name is a line from the French movie 'Girl on the Bridge,' about a knife thrower who persuades suicidal girls to be his assistants.❞

Do you just throw knives at your assistants?

❝I throw knives, tomahawks, axes, and machetes—but I never throw 'at,' I throw 'around!' My assistant stands in front of a board, or is strapped on to the Wheel of Death while I throw two knives per revolution, one on each side of her. I also catch knives mid-air, and throw both right- and left-handed, blindfolded, and with my back to the board. I don't know why they call it 'impalement arts' because the last thing we want to do is impale our assistants.❞

How fast can you throw?

❝Throwing a single knife at a time, I can throw 75 in one minute. Throwing three knives at a time, my personal best is 144 knives around my partner in one minute.❞

Do you have any special techniques?

❝I video what I do and watch it back—I study my hands very carefully. When I throw blind, I use sound to judge where to throw. My assistant sets me up facing the board, and I know exactly where she's standing.❞

Have you ever injured yourself or an assistant?

❝I once had to stop because I stuck myself with the point of a knife and started bleeding from my fingers. Knives have bounced from the Wheel of Death and scraped the girl, but I've never impaled a girl.❞

Is it difficult to find willing assistants?

❝Very! I don't just want a girl to stand there as my target—it's about the way she flirts with me and the audience, while facing danger.❞

Do you come from a performing family?

❝Through my high school years I was a gymnast. I competed in the junior Olympics. One of my daughters is a surgeon who is very good with a knife in a different way! My wife Barbara was a knife thrower herself but retired—she has no wish to be my assistant.❞

Mini Chain
These toothpicks have 28 chainlinks carved into each of them. They were made by Mallikarjun Reddy from Bangalore, India, in 2005.

ACTUAL SIZE!

Just for Laughs
In 1992, American comedian Mike Heeman set out to tell as many jokes as possible in 24 hours. By the end of his marathon gag-fest, he had cracked no fewer than 12,682 jokes.

Riding High
In June 2004, Terry Goertzen, a pastor from Winnipeg, Canada, completed a 328-yd (300-m) ride on a bicycle constructed like a ladder that stood 18 ft 2½ in (5.5 m) high and was powered by a chain measuring 35 ft 8 in (11 m) in length.

Mass Pillow Fight
No fewer than 766 people knocked the stuffing out of each other at Oregon State University in 2003 in a mammoth pillow fight. The event was organized by student Lige Armstrong as part of a class project.

Math Marvel
A 59-year-old man from Chiba, Japan, recited pi—or the ratio of the circumference of a circle to its diameter—to over 80,000 decimal places during a 12-hour challenge in 2005. Akira Haraguchi started the attempt shortly after noon on July 1 and stopped at 83,431 decimal places early the following day. In doing so, he comfortably beat his previous best of 54,000 decimal places.

Balloon Bonanza
In a bizarre challenge, students from Temasek Secondary School in Singapore set out to produce as many objects shaped from balloons as possible. In July 2005, a huge gathering of 1,471 students exercised their lungs to create 16,380 balloons in shapes that ranged from flowers to giraffes.

Super Bowl
Suresh Joachim created bowling history in Toronto, Ontario, in June 2005, by bowling nonstop without sleep for 100 hours. To meet his challenge, he endured 360 games of bowling in which he achieved a fantastic 120 strikes. However, he also managed to break nine bowling balls!

In Peak Condition

On May 21, 2004, Pemba Dorjie Sherpa, a 27-year-old Nepali, climbed the upper reaches of the world's highest mountain, Mount Everest, in just 8 hours 10 minutes. Everest is 29,039 ft (8,851 m) high and Pemba's climb—from base camp at 17,380 ft (5,297 m) to the summit—usually takes experienced mountaineers three to four days.

In September 1998, **1,000 students** from the University of *Guelph* in Ontario, Canada, formed an enormous human conveyor belt— passing a *surfboard* along the belt's entire length.

Wild Bill's Bike

When William "Wild Bill" Gelbke decided to build a giant motorcycle at a Chicago workshop, he had no plans or blueprints. It took him eight long years, but when the Roadog finally appeared in 1965, it created quite a stir. The mammoth bike measured 17 ft (5.2 m) in length, weighed 3,280 lb (1,488 kg), had a frame built from aircraft tubing, and had a cruising speed of a cool 90 mph (145 km/h).

Lawnmower Ride

As part of the Keep America Beautiful campaign, Brad Hauter, from Indiana, rode a lawnmower coast to coast across the U.S.A. He set off from San Francisco in April 2003 and arrived in New York 79 days later after a journey of more than 5,600 mi (9,012 km). The specially adapted mower had a top speed of 25 mph (40 km/h).

Full House

Believe it or not, 15,756 players took part in a single game of bingo at the Canadian National Exhibition in August 1983.

Human Ramp

Tim Cridland's feats are inspired by the mystics of the Far East. Through using "mind-over-matter" philosophy, he has taught his brain not to register the feeling of pain. He can swallow swords and dance on broken glass, but it is his car feat that he counts as his greatest achievement. While lying on a bed of nails with spikes 5 in (13 cm) long, he is able to endure the weight of a 1-ton car driving over him. His skin is not even punctured.

Basketball Marathon

At New England's Beatrice High School gym between July 28 and July 30, 2005, players staged a 52-hour marathon basketball game. "Everyone was exhausted by the end of the game," said organizer Jim Weeks. Some players struggled through the early hours of the mornings and were ready to give up when they reached 40 hours, but they bravely battled on. The final score was 7,935 points to 6,963.

Monster Board

In 1996, Todd Swank from San Diego, California, built a skateboard for himself and his friends that was 10 ft (3 m) long, 4 ft (1.2 m) wide, and 3 ft (1 m) high. It weighed 500 lb (227 kg) and used tires from a sports car. He said he wanted to create a skateboard that no one would ever forget.

Reading Aloud

In March 2005, 1,544 students from Pleasant Valley Middle School, Pocono, Pennsylvania, simultaneously read aloud *Oh the Places You'll Go* by Dr. Seuss.

Inflated Lizard

If attacked, the chuckwalla, one of the largest lizards in the U.S., will crawl into a space between two rocks and puff itself up with air so that it can't be pulled out. It can inflate its lungs to increase its body size by as much as 50 per cent.

49-Day Fast

CHEN JIANMIN, a 50-year-old doctor of Traditional Chinese Medicine, went 49 days without food in 2004, drinking only water.

An exponent of the practice of fasting, Chen entered the sealed glass cabin, measuring 160 sq ft (15 sq m), on March 20, 2004. The box was fixed 30 ft (9 m) high above the ground on a mountainside near Ya'an City. More than 10,000 visitors who turned out to watch the fast could see into Mr. Chen's house, except for two areas where he showered and used the toilet. While doing so he had to keep his head above a curtain to prove that he wasn't eating. Chen entered the box weighing 123 lb (56 kg) and emerged from the box at least 33 lb (15 kg) lighter. He claimed to have once gone 81 days without food.

Chen takes a call. He claimed to have answered more than 8,000 telephone calls from all over China while in his box.

Suspended 30 ft (9 m) above the ground, Chen sits in his glass box watched over by his team below.

Chen pours himself a drink of water inside his box, which was equipped with items such as a fan, table, chairs, and electric power.

Clever Kids

★ Born in 1982, Anthony McQuone from Weybridge, England, could speak Latin and quote Shakespeare when he was just two years old.

★ David Farragut, who later served as a naval officer during the American Civil War, was given command of his first ship when just 12 years old.

★ American singer Tori Amos began to play the piano at 2 years of age and wrote her first song when she was just five years old.

★ Romanian painter Alexandra Nechita had her first solo exhibition in 1993 at the age of eight at a library in Los Angeles, California.

Ding-Dong Merrily

Canadian choir leader Joe Defries had music ringing in his ears after playing the handbells for nearly 28 hours straight. Joe, from Abbotsford, British Columbia, has been playing the handbells for more than 25 years and drew up a list of 1,300 tunes for his marathon solo venture in July 2005. Although he had never previously gone beyond 8 hours of solo ringing, Joe rose to the challenge, even finding time to crack jokes in the 30-second breaks he took after each tune.

Horror Crawl

Colorado Springs students Leo Chau and Sean Duffy crawled on their hands and knees for an agonizing 32 mi (51.5 km) through hailstorms and lightning in June 2005 to raise money for charity. The tortuous 44-hour crawl took its toll. Duffy suffered hallucinations and motion sickness while Chau was struck by severe dehydration.

On a Roll

In May 2005, to raise money for the Asian tsunami relief fund, students at the Cornell School of Hotel Administration, New York State, created a huge spring roll 1,315 ft (400 m) long. The monster hors d'oeuvre contained 3,500 spring-roll wrappers, 400 lbs (180 kg) of vermicelli noodles, 250 lbs (113 kg) each of carrots and cucumbers, and 80 lbs (36 kg) of lettuce.

Speed Juggling

Shawn McCue from Sedalia, Missouri, was surfing the Internet when he came across a site for speed juggling. In high school he had been able to bounce a soccer ball on his foot as many as 600 times in three minutes, so he resolved to recreate past glories. In July 2005, in Jefferson City, he performed 155 juggles in 30 seconds, maintaining perfect balance throughout, while the ball never once rose more than 1 in (2.5 cm) off his foot.

▶ **Super Boy**
Eleven-year-old Bruce Khlebnikov tows an airplane with a rope attached to his hair on May 24, 2001, in Moscow, Russia. He has also pulled cars, lifted Russia's heaviest bodybuilder, torn thick books in half, and used his fists to break 15 ceramic plates that were attached together.

Whole Lotta Shakin'

While campaigning in Albuquerque for election as New Mexico's governor in September 2002, Bill Richardson, a former U.S. Ambassador to the United Nations, shook 13,392 hands in 8 hours, smashing President Theodore Roosevelt's previously esteemed total of 8,513. At the end of the gruelling session, Richardson immediately sunk his hand into ice.

High Tea

Dressed in formal evening wear, three explorers climbed into a hot-air balloon in June 2005 for an airborne dinner party. David Hempleman-Adams, Bear Grylls, and Alan Veal soared to a height of 24,262 ft (7,395 m) above Bath, England. Then, Grylls and Veal climbed 40 ft (12 m) down to a platform where, at a neatly laid dinner table, they ate asparagus spears followed by poached salmon and a terrine of summer fruits, all served in specially designed warm boxes to combat the freezing temperatures at altitude.

Waist Spinner

Ashrita Furman successfully hula hoops with a hoop that is 14 ft 7½ in (4.46 m) in diameter in New York's Flushing Meadow Park on July 15, 2005.

Elvis Lives!

They were all shook up in July 2005 in Cleveland, Ohio, when a total of 106 Elvis impersonators gathered on a high-school football field and performed a three-minute rendition of "Viva Las Vegas." Men, women, and children alike all donned gold shades and black plastic wigs for the occasion.

Bumper Bagel

For the 2004 New York State Fair, Bruegger's Bakeries created a bagel that weighed 868 lbs (394 kg) and measured 6 ft (1.8 m) in diameter.

Jumping for Joy

Gary Stewart, of Ohio, made 177,737 consecutive jumps on a pogo stick in 20 hours in May 1990.

Chocolate Delight

Pastry cook Ugo Mignone is seen here working on a Christmas display made entirely of chocolate at a cake workshop in Naples, Italy, in November 2004. Twenty Neapolitan pastry chefs, using a huge 6,600 lbs (3,000 kg) of chocolate, worked to create this tasty nativity scene.

The mouthwatering chocolate nativity receives its finishing touches.

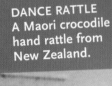

DANCE RATTLE
A Maori crocodile hand rattle from New Zealand.

OPENED IN 1970, the first Gatlinburg museum was destroyed by fire in 1992. Reopened the following year, the new museum was built as if crumbling during a severe earthquake. Gatlinburg has many exhibits, including a Mastodon skeleton, Yeti hair, and a giraffe made out of coat hangers.

BOTTLED ARROW
These wooden arrows were inserted through the bottle without any cutting or gluing!

FUTURISTIC ROBOT
Created by Simon Blades, this robot is made entirely from used automobile parts.

DON'T MISS!

▶ Extinct elephant bird egg

▶ World's largest gum wrapper chain

▶ Elephant jaw

▶ Fiji mermaid

▶ Berlin Wall

▶ Wood carved Vespa motorcycle

▶ Egyptian mummy

▶ Giant punt gun

▶ Car parts robot soldier

TALLEST MAN
When Robert Wadlow died in 1940, at the age of 22, he was 8 ft 11 in (2.7 m) tall, weighed 440 lbs (200 kg), wore a size 37AA shoe, and had a 25 ring size.

MASTODON SKELETON
Robert Ripley watches over this mastodon, a prehistoric relative of the elephant discovered beneath a golf course in Ohio.

Robert L. Ripley 1893-1949

KUGEL BALL
Weighing 10,518 lb (4,770 kg), this ball can amazingly be moved by the touch of a finger.

SHRUNKEN HEAD
The Jivaro tribe of Ecuador claimed their enemies' heads as war trophies.

TWO-HEADED GOAT
Each head has a trachea and esophagus, but each leads to only one lung.

Snow Boat

An amazing sculpture of an ancient warship was carved out of snow and ice in the city of Jilin, China, in January 2005. It was 82 ft (25 m) long, 20 ft (6 m) wide, and 30 ft (9.1 m) high.

Night Skiing

Canadians Ralph Hildebrand and Dave Phillips water-skied for 56 hours 35 minutes around Rocky Point, British Columbia, in June 1994. They used spotlights and infrared binoculars during the night-time periods of the marathon.

Property Giant

The game of Monopoly was played on this huge board in Berlin in June 2005. To make a move, the pieces had to be lifted by two players!

Fish Swallower

In just one hour in July 2005, Indian yoga teacher G.P. Vijaya Kumar swallowed 509 small fish through his mouth and blew them out of his nose! Kumar was inspired by American Kevin Cole, who blows spaghetti strands out of a nostril in a single blow. After successfully ejecting peas and corn through his nose in earlier exhibitions, Kumar turned to live fish.

VicTORY To ReLish

FOR THE FIFTH straight year, it was a moment for Takeru Kobayashi to relish when he consumed 49 hot dogs in just 12 minutes!

In 2005, the 27-year-old speed eater from Nagano, Japan, retained his crown at Nathan's Famous Fourth of July International Hot Dog Eating Contest at Coney Island, New York. Kobayashi, who stands 5 ft 7 in (1.7 m) tall and weighs just 144 lbs (65 kg), beat runner-up Sonya Thomas of Alexandria, Virginia, by 12 hot dogs, enabling the coveted Mustard Yellow Belt to return to Japan for the ninth year out of the past ten. Kobayashi's personal best was a staggering $53\frac{1}{2}$ hot dogs in 12 minutes!

A brief moment before Takeru Kobayashi's success, he is seen struggling to keep his mouth closed as he valiantly attempts to chew and swallow his 49th hot dog.

Nailed Down

Lee Graber of Tallmadge, Ohio, was sandwiched between two beds of nails with a weight of 1,659 lbs (752.5 kg) pressing on top of him for 10 seconds in June 2000. The weight was lowered into position by a crane.

Tree Planter

Ken Chaplin planted 15,170 trees in a single day near Prince Albert, Saskatchewan, on June 30, 2001.

Highly Strung

In June 2000, a team of 11 students from the Academy of Science and Technology at Woodlands, Texas, and their physics teacher, Scott Rippetoe, unveiled a fully playable Flying V guitar that measured 43 ft 7½ in (13.2 m) long and 16ft 5½ in (5 m) wide. It weighed 2,244 lbs (1,018 kg) and used strings that were 8 in (20 cm) thick and 25 ft (7.6 m) in length.

⏷ Danny's Way

Daredevil American skateboarder Danny Way created history in 2005 by clearing the Great Wall of China without motorized assistance. He hurtled down a 120-ft (36.5-m) specially constructed vertical ramp at a speed of approximately 50 mph (80 km/h) and leapt a 61-ft (19-m) gap to land safely on a ramp erected on the other side of the wall. The 31-year-old from Encinitas, California, spent eight months planning the two-second jump.

Mime Master

Bulgarian mime artist Alexander Iliev performed a 24-hour mime in July 2001 at the Golden Sands resort near Varna, Bulgaria, pausing for only a one-minute break every hour. His marathon effort featured more than 400 different pantomime pieces and saw him cover around 140 mi (225 km) on stage.

Jai Narain Bhati, a barber from *Bhopal*, India, cut the hair of 1,451 people over a 108-hour period in January 2002. His only breaks were for 10 minutes every hour.

Toga Parade

In August 2003, in the town of Cottage Grove, Oregon, 2,166 people dressed in togas paraded down Main Street re-enacting the parade scene from the movie *National Lampoon's Animal House*, which had been filmed in the town in 1977.

Maggot Bath

Christine Martin of Horsham, England, sat in a bathtub of maggots for 1 hour 30 minutes in 2002.

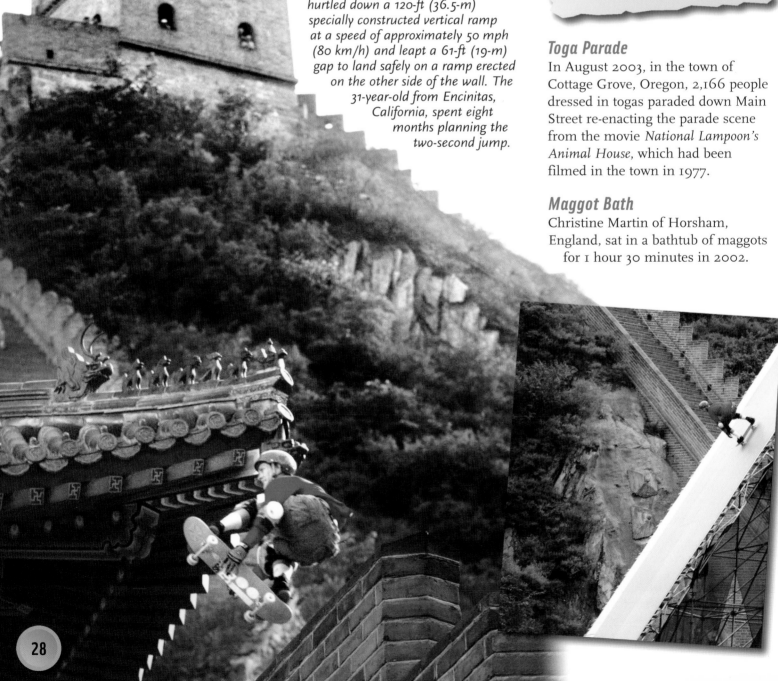

Brick It Up
Terry Cole balances 75 bricks weighing a staggering 328 lbs (148.8 kg) on his head. Among other things, he has also carried a single brick held downward for 72 mi (116 km) and balanced 16 bricks on his chin!

Dog Tired
Andrew Larkey tried to walk 19 dogs simultaneously in Sydney, Australia, in May 2005. He began by being pulled in 19 directions before controlling 11 of the dogs single-handedly over the ⅔-mi (1-km) walk.

Coffin Ordeal
In May 2005 in Louisville, Kentucky, escapologist Aron Houdini (his legal name) spent an amazing 79 minutes inside a sealed coffin with no air. He was handcuffed, leg-cuffed, and chained inside the coffin. "I freaked out at first," admitted Houdini, who was able to communicate with his crew by way of a radio from inside the wooden box. "However, once I got my mind under control, I started what I had been practicing for almost a year. I slowed my metabolism down and then I concentrated on resting."

Stone Skipper
For years the leading exponent of the art of skipping a stone across the water was an American called Jerdone Coleman-McGhee. In 1994, he achieved 38 skips from a bridge on the Blanco River in Texas.

Wurst is Best
In June 2005, 80 cooks from Leipzig, Germany, created a sausage that was 108 ft (33 m) long and required 294 broilers (grills) to cook it. The attempt to broil the sausage had to be called off when gusts of wind scattered the burning charcoal.

Eye-watering
Brian Duffield from Newent, U.K., chewed and consumed a whole onion weighing 7.5 oz (212 g) in 1 minute 32 seconds. He said: "The hardest thing is actually swallowing it. You just have to get it down." A keen gardener, Brian grows his own onions and uses them for practice.

Group Hug
In April 2004, a staggering total of 5,117 students, staff, and friends from St. Matthew Catholic High School, Orleans, Ontario, joined forces—and arms!—to have an enormous group hug.

Tightrope Crossing

Age was no bar to American acrobat, balloonist, and tightrope-walker William Ivy Baldwin. During his lifetime, he made 87 tightrope crossings of the South Boulder Canyon, Colorado—the first when he was 14 and the last on July 31, 1948, his 82nd birthday! The wire was 320 ft (97.5 m) long and the drop was a terrifying 125 ft (38 m).

Aerial Wedding

Nobody in the world has done more skydives than Don Kellner. Don from Hazleton, Pennsylvania, has over 36,000 skydives to his name and his wife Darlene is no slouch either, having made around 13,000. Naturally enough, their wedding in 1990 was conducted in mid-air, the ceremony being performed by fellow skydiver, the Rev. Dave Sangley.

Inside Job

In April 2005, a British couple drove the length of Europe without getting out of their car. Dr. James Shippen and Barbara May, from Bromsgrove, England, made the 2,000-mi (3,200-km) journey from John O'Groats, on the northern coast of Scotland, to the southern tip of Italy to demonstrate their invention, the Indipod, an in-car toilet.

Believe it or not, in **May 2004**, **927 students** and **staff** at Taylor University, Indiana, *leaped* over each other in a mammoth exhibition of **leapfrogging!**

Handcycle Tour

In 2005, paraplegic Andreas Dagelet set out from Coochiemudlo Island, Brisbane, to circumnavigate Australia on a handcycle—a sort of bicycle that is powered by arms and hands instead of legs and feet. The entire journey measured approximately 10,600 mi (17,000 km).

Self-taught Cowboy

There aren't too many cowboys in Maryland, but Andy Rotz is an exception. The self-taught cowboy from Hagerstown—who learned his art from watching John Wayne and Clint Eastwood movies—can do over 11,000 Texas skips, a maneuver that entails whipping a vertical loop of rope from side to side while jumping through the middle. He had to keep the rope spinning for 3 hours 10 minutes and perform a skip roughly every second.

Chorus Line

In 2005, 15,785 workers in Tangshan City, China, all sang "Workers are Strong" simultaneously.

▶ Baby Bike

Bobby Hunt (aka Circus Boy) reckons he has spent over $1,500 on building and fixing his bike—and it's only 3 in (7.6 cm) long, axel to axel, and 7³/₄ in (20 cm) tall. The bike's size might be a problem, but Bobby rides it with ease, and can even perform wheelies.

Open Wide

Jim Mouth is a comedy entertainer based in Las Vegas who has been performing incredible stunts for more than 20 years. These often involve putting absolutely *anything* in his mouth!

When did you get started—and why do you keep going?

"My first stunt, when I was about 29, was playing drums for two weeks non stop. I had to drink lots of coffee to stay awake! I'm 51 now, and my comedy shows are more of a full-time thing, but my biggest drive is to use stunts to raise money for charity. "

What is your most famous stunt?

"I like doing the "most cigarettes in the mouth" stunt. I'm up to 159 cigarettes now. I've performed this on TV many times. I put all the cigarettes in apart from one which the host of the show puts in. Then they light them with two propane torches, I cough and wheeze for about three minutes, then spit them out. I'm dizzy for about half an hour afterwards. One time I coughed out about 100 cigarettes—the crazy thing is I'm actually a non-smoker. I've actually done this stunt on non-smoking days to support people giving up cigarettes. "

Do you have a special technique?

"Before a stunt I wedge corks into my mouth to stretch my lips, but my real secret is that I can dislocate my jaw. I didn't know I was doing it until they X-rayed me on a TV show last year. All I knew was that it was painful and made my eyes water! "

What other stunts do you do?

"Mouth stunts include smoking 41 cigars at once, and 41 pipes. We once had a whole band playing music under the water in a pool, and another time I sat on every seat in the University of Michigan football stadium, the biggest in the United States. There were 101,701 seats—it took me 96 hours and 12 minutes, and four pairs of pants! "

How dangerous are your stunts?

"Apparently when my jaw dislocates it rests on my larynx, which could suffocate me. No one will insure me! "

Is there anything you would not do?

"Because I play drums I really don't want to break a finger or an arm. But I will put up with anything in my mouth—I might try keeping a tarantula spider in my mouth for half an hour. "

How long will you carry on?

"My goal is to do one stunt every year for at least the next ten years. One I've got in the pipeline is "most hats on the head"—I'm aiming for a stack of 300, which will be about 8½ ft tall and weigh about 110 lb. I'll probably retire when I'm in my sixties—I'll do 170 cigarettes and then call it a day. "

Climbing High

★ Czech climber Martin Tlusty survived a terrifying 1,000-ft (305-m) fall down the side of a mountain in Slovakia in 2005.

★ Swiss authorities wrap some mountain glaciers with aluminum foil in the summertime to stop them from melting.

★ Frenchman Christian Taillefer cycled down a glacier at 132 mph (212 km/h) in Vars, France, in 1998.

★ When Mount St. Helens in Washington State, the highest peak in the U.S.A., erupted spectacularly in 1980, the avalanche on the north slope reached incredible speeds of 250 mph (400 km/h).

Rocketman

Texan Eric Scott took to the skies in England in April 2004, rocketing upward to 152 ft (46 m)—the height of a 12-story building. Eric remained airborne for 26 seconds. His "rocketbelt" was mounted on a fiberglass corset with two rocket nozzles and a belt that had basic controls for steering.

Biker Duo

American couple Chris and Erin Ratay covered 101,322 mi (163,058 km) on separate motorcycles during a journey that took them through 50 countries on six different continents. They set off from Morocco in May 1999 and arrived home in New York in August 2003.

Internet Marathon

In November 1997, Canada's Daniel Messier spent 103 hours nonstop surfing the internet—that's more than four days!

Giant Noodle

Believe it or not, participants at Canada's Corso Italia Toronto Fiesta in 2003 created a spaghetti noodle that was an amazing 525 ft (160 m) long.

Sore Hands

Peter Schoenfeld of Ontario, Canada, chopped 209 wooden blocks by hand in just two minutes in October 2001.

Making Whoopee

In July 2005, following a baseball game in Bowie, Maryland, an incredible 4,439 Bowie Baysox fans sat on whoopee cushions simultaneously to create a gargantuan flatulence sound!

Lengthy Lecture

Errol Muzawazi, a lecturer from Zimbabwe, delivered a lecture at the age of 20 lasting for 88 hours in 2005, talking nonstop for more than three days. His audience at Jagellonian University in Krakow, Poland, fell asleep!

Quick Solution

If you need help with math, ask Gert Mittring. The 38-year-old needed just 11.8 seconds to calculate the 13th root of a 100-digit number in his head during a special challenge near Frankfurt, Germany, in 2004. He even solved the problem faster than onlookers with electric calculators.

In Flight

Australian professional golfer Stuart Appleby drives off on one of the runways at Sydney Airport, Australia, on November 22, 2004. Appleby was competing against fellow golfers in a golf driving distance contest, which he won with a massive shot that reached an incredible distance of 2,069 ft 3 in (630.58 m)— over one-third of a mile.

On a Sydney Airport runway, Appleby makes his golf ball fly.

Sundae Best

On July 24, 1988, a giant ice-cream sundae was made by Palm Dairies of Alberta, Canada. It featured an amazing 44,689 lbs (20,270 kg) of ice cream, 9,688 lbs 2 oz (4,394 kg) of syrup, and 537 lbs 3 oz (244 kg) of toppings!

Balancing Act

At the age of 12, Tim Johnston, of Piedmont, California, balanced 15 spoons on his face for 30 seconds in May 2004.

Corset Cathie

Cathie Jung, now aged 72, has been wearing a corset, even when asleep, for over 20 years. At 5 ft 6 in (1.68 m) tall and weighing 135 lbs (61 kg), her waist measures a tiny 15 in (38 cm). The only time Cathie removes the corset is when she showers. Cathie's corset training started with a 26-in (66-cm) corset in 1983, when she had a 28-in (71-cm) waist. She gradually reduced the size of the corsets as they became comfortable.

Freestyle Rap

Toronto rapper D.O. performed a freestyle rap that went on for 8 hours 45 minutes in July 2003.

In what was an **enormous gathering** of Christmas carolers, **519** hardy souls braved the New York cold for a mass sing-along on the steps of Manhattan's General Post Office in December 2003.

Having a Ball

David Ogron has a ball every day of his life. In fact, in an average year he has 400,000 balls. The Californian hit on his unusual career some years ago when he was practicing with friends on the golf range. "We were seeing who could hit the ball the fastest. That's when I realized I had a talent." With the help of ball-setter Scott "Speedy" McKinney, who puts each ball on the tee, Ogron hit 1,388 balls in 30 minutes in May 2005 at Louisville, Kentucky. And in July 2005, he hit 82 in one minute in Miami. On another occasion, he hit 10,392 balls in 24 hours.

Index

ACKNOWLEDGMENTS

COVER (t/l) Deborah Ann Duschl, (b/l) Laure A. Leber, (t/r) Jim Mouth, (b/r) Ando Art; 6–7 Norm Betts/Rex Features; 8 James Bodington/ Reuters; 9 (t & c/r) John Gress/Reuters, (b/l) Arko Datta/Getty Images; 10 (t) Reuters, (b) Konstantin Postnikov/Camera Press/ITAR/TASS; 11 Deborah Ann Duschl; 12–13 (dp) Ando Art; 12 (t/r) Aamir Qureshi/AFP/Getty Images, (c) Ando Art; 13 (t/r) Rex Features, (c/r) Ando Art; 14 (t) Historical PhotoArchive Collection/Niagara Falls Public Library; 16 (c/l & b/l) Caricato/Rex Features, (r) Vano Shlamov/Getty Images; 17 (t/r) Laure A. Leber, (b/l) Dale Rio; 18 (t) Dibyangshu Sarkar/AFP/Getty Images, (b) J.P. Moczulski /Reuters; 20 (b/l & r) China Photos/Reuters; 21 Sipa Press/Rex Features; 22 East News/Getty Images; 23 (t & c) Shannon Stapleton/Reuters, (b) Alessia Pierdomenico/Reuters; 26 (t) China Newsphoto/Reuters, (c/r & b) Tobias Schwarz/Reuters; 27 Seth Wenig/Reuters; 28 China Newsphoto/Reuters; 29 (t) Michael Fresco/ Rex Features, (b) Anthony Devlin/Rex Features; 30 Bobby Hunt; 31 Jim Mouth; 32 Rex Features; 33 (b/l) Emily Baron/Barcroft Media, (t/r) Tim Winborne/Reuters

All other photos are from Corel, PhotoDisc, Digital Vision and Ripley's Entertainment Inc.